I CAN BE A

FARMER

By Kathy Henderson

Prepared under the direction of Robert Hillerich, Ph.D.

 CHILDRENS PRESS®

CHICAGO

Library of Congress Cataloging-in-Publication Data

Henderson, Kathy. 1949-
   I can be a farmer / by Kathy Henderson.
      p.   cm.
   Summary: Describes, in simple text, the work of a farmer.
   ISBN 0-516-01923-6
   1. Agriculture—Juvenile literature. 2. Farmers—Juvenile
literature. 3. Farm life—Juvenile literature. (1. Farmers.
2. Occupations.) I. Title
S519.H46   1989
630—dc19

88.3716
CIP
AC

PICTURE DICTIONARY

livestock farmer

livestock   veterinarian

crop farmer

crops

citrus fruit trees

smudge pot

grains

fertilizer

tractor

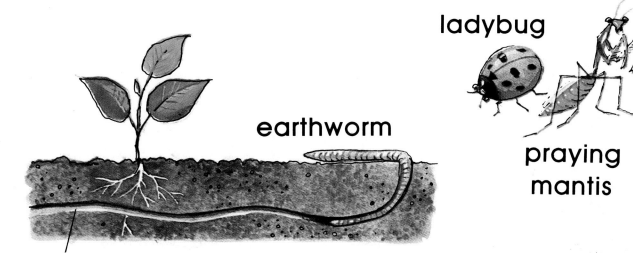

earthworm

ladybug

praying mantis

air tunnel

flood

drought

protective clothing

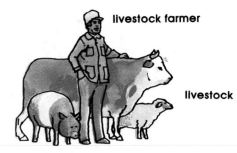

livestock farmer

livestock

Do you enjoy working outdoors? Do you like helping things grow?

For some people, growing things is their job. They are called farmers.

Would you like to be a farmer?

There are many kinds of farmers. Some grow animals. They are called livestock farmers.

Feeding dairy calves (left) and feeding baby goats (right)

Livestock farmers are up
before dawn. They feed
their animals. They milk the
cows and goats. They
gather eggs from nests.
Finally the farmer can eat
breakfast. The cows and
goats will be milked again
in the evening.

Children who live on farms have their own farm chores. Even a small child can milk a cow (above left). The boy on the right is feeding goats and a llama. The child below is sorting eggs by their sizes.

Cornstalks on this dairy farm are being cut and chopped for cattle feed.

During the day, livestock
farmers may grow crops
like hay, corn, and oats to
feed their animals. They
clean barns and spread
the manure on the fields
to help fertilize the soil.

Above left: A machine mixes animal feed; the feed will be put into bags.
Above right: A brother and sister feed hay to their Holstein cows.
Below left: This farmer is harvesting long rows of corn in the autumn.
Below right: A threshing machine works through a field of oats.

A livestock farmer
checks on the animals
several times a day to
make sure they are all
healthy. An animal about
to give birth needs special
care. Sometimes the
farmer helps deliver the
baby animal.

This is how a veterinarian gives a pill to a cow.

If an animal gets sick, the farmer calls a veterinarian, or animal doctor. The farmer works with the veterinarian to help the animal get better. The farmer must keep careful records about all of the animals.

veterinarian

Left: Harvesting a leafy green vegetable called escarole
Right: Freshly-harvested potatoes are loaded into a sack.

crop farmer

crops

A farmer who grows crops instead of animals is called a crop farmer. Some crop farmers grow vegetables such as carrots, lettuce, potatoes, onions, and broccoli.

Some of the crops are sold fresh for customers to

Farmers may bring their crops to a farmer's market, where people can buy the vegetables and fruits while they are fresh.

eat right away. But most of the vegetables are sold to companies that will can or freeze them. That way, the vegetables will not spoil before they can be eaten.

How many other kinds of vegetables can you name that farmers grow?

Harvesting corn (left) and wheat (right)

grains

Some crop farmers grow grains such as oats, corn, or wheat. Some grow crops like soybeans or navy beans. This type of crop is not harvested until the seed has started to dry and the stalk is dead. After harvesting, the seeds

are put in special bins.
There, hot air is fanned
through pipes to finish
drying the seeds so they
won't spoil.

Later the grain and
beans are sold to make
cereals, bread, and other
products.

Left: A woman picking strawberries
Right: A young farmer checking fruit in his peach orchard

Fruit is another crop that farmers grow. Some fruits, such as strawberries, grow on ground-hugging plants. Other fruits, such as blueberries, grow on bushes. Cherries, apples, and pears grow on trees in the farmer's orchard.

Citrus fruits, such as oranges and lemons, are grown in areas where the climate stays warm most of the time. If the weather turns cold, farmers light "smudge pots" in the orchard or grove to help keep the fruit from freezing.

citrus fruit trees

smudge pot

Top: An airplane
sprays a bug killer
(insecticide) on
some crops.
Above and far
right: Farm workers
wearing
protective
clothing
Right: A harmful
caterpillar
destroys the leaf
of a cotton plant.

fertilizer

tractor

Farmers use special fertilizers to help the plants grow. Sometimes they use chemicals to keep away weeds and bugs that might damage the growing plants.

Many of the chemicals and fertilizers used on the farm are dangerous if not used properly. Farmers often wear heavy gloves, air masks, and other protective clothing when using these chemicals.

protective clothing

19

A praying mantis, the farmer's friend

Not all bugs are harmful.
Praying mantises and
ladybugs feed on
plant-eating insects.
Farmers also rely on
earthworms to burrow
through the soil and
create tiny air tunnels.

ladybug

praying mantis

earthworm

air
tunnel

Special farm
equipment for
harvesting celery
(left) and
harvesting barley
(right)

These tunnels help the
plant's roots to breathe.
Farmers use special
equipment to plant,
cultivate, and harvest their
crops. They must know
how to handle and care
for these machines.

Left: A team of
horses pulls a plow
in the old style of
farming.
Right: An antique
steam tractor

tractor

Many years ago,
farmers used horses and
oxen to help them plow
and prepare the soil. Most
of the planting and tilling
was done by hand.
Today, most farmers use
tractors and other
machines to help them
farm larger areas faster
and better.

There are many different kinds of farm machines and equipment. Each has a special purpose. Here are farm machines for harvesting barley and planting soybeans (above left), picking cotton (above right), planting corn seed (below left), and harvesting corn (below right).

This cotton farmer is using a computer to predict the way his crop will develop.

Nowadays even computers are used on the farm. For instance, computers can be programmed to feed animals at a certain time

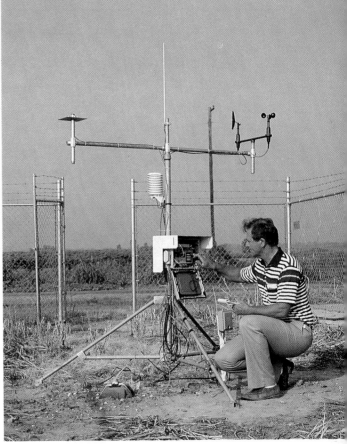

These farmers use special devices for controlling irrigation sprinklers (above) and collecting weather information (right).

of the day. Computers also help farmers keep crop records, bookkeeping records, and other information up to date.

A student on a research farm at a large state university

Some farmers have
studied agricultural
science in college. Still,
most farmers learn about
farming by growing up or
working on a farm. Young

Top left: A rancher teaches a boy how to handle a horse. Bottom left: Farm boys compete in a Future Farmers of America contest. Right: A farm boy tends his prize-winning cow at a county fair.

people can learn more about farming through a 4-H club or Future Farmers of America.

Dairy farmers walk toward their barn at dawn for the morning milking of their cows.

Caring for animals and planting and harvesting crops is easier to do now than in the past. Still, farmers must be willing to work long, hard hours all year long in many kinds of weather to get their job done.

Farming can be dangerous work. It is risky,

Left: Parched soil
during a drought
Right: A lush and
fertile farm

too. Bad weather such as a flood or drought can kill an entire crop. Disease can make animals sick.

But farmers accept these risks because they enjoy working outdoors. They like helping things grow.

flood

drought

WORDS YOU SHOULD KNOW

bookkeeping (BOOK • keep • ing)—keeping the business accounts and records of a company

citrus fruits (SIT • rus FROOTS)—sharp-tasting fruits with a thick rind and pulpy flesh, usually grown in warm climates

climate (KLY • mit)—the usual weather conditions in a certain area

drought (DROWT)—a long period of dry weather that damages crops or slows their growth

fertilize (FUR • til • yze)—to make plants grow better by adding chemicals or manure to the soil

flood (FLUHD)—the overflowing of a body of water onto dry land

4-H club—a club in which young people learn useful skills in farming, conservation, handcrafts, and many other areas; the four H's stand for head, heart, hands, and health

Future Farmers of America—a club that helps high school students prepare for careers in agriculture

grains (GRAYNS)—grass-like plants that produce starchy seeds used in making cereals and breads

harvest (HAR • vest)—to gather in or pick crops

livestock (LYV • stock)—farm animals that produce useful products or do farm work

manure (muh • NOO • ur)—waste matter from livestock, used to fertilize crops

orchard (OR • churd)—an area where fruit trees or nut trees are planted

oxen (OX • un)—plural of ox, a large animal used to carry heavy loads or pull farm equipment

smudge pot (SMUJ POT)—a container with oil burning in the bottom; the smoke serves as a blanket to protect fruit trees from cold weather

till—to plow the soil, sow seed, and raise crops

veterinarian (vet • er • in • AIR • ee • un)—a doctor who takes care of animals

INDEX

About the Author

Kathy Henderson is Executive Director of the National Association for Young Writers, vice president of the NAYW Board of Trustees, and Michigan Advisor for the Society of Children's Book Writers. She works closely with children, teachers, and librarians through young author conferences and workshops, and is a frequent guest speaker in schools. An experienced freelance writer with hundreds of newspaper and magazine articles to her credit, she is also the author of the *Market Guide for Young Writers*. Mrs. Henderson lives on a 400-acre dairy farm in Michigan with her husband, Keith, and two teenage children.